CHRISSIE
The Curious Christmas Cassowary

Balboa Press books may be ordered through booksellers or by contacting:

Balboa Press
A Division of Hay House
1663 Liberty Drive
Bloomington, IN 47403
www.balboapress.com
1 (877) 407-4847

ISBN: 978-1-5043-0588-4 (sc)
ISBN: 978-1-5043-0589-1 (e)

Print information available on the last page.

Balboa Press rev. date: 10/17/2018

BALBOA
PRESS
A DIVISION OF HAY HOUSE

CHRISSIE
The Curious Christmas Cassowary

KRISTINA CONE
ILLUSTRATED BY : LYLE JAKOSALEM

HOORAY! It was Christmas time at last. Chrissie the young cassowary had been waiting for this special time for so long. It was a clear, warm, sunny, blue-sky day in a pretty place called Mission Beach in North Queensland, Australia. Mission Beach was situated in between two bigger cities called Cairns and Townsville and was Chrissie's home. She lived here in amongst the leafy, green, tangly rainforest with her family: her Daddy, Clementine Cassowary, her bigger brother Calvin and her two younger sisters Claire and Cassy. Their Grandfather Clem, lived just near them too. The chicks all loved his interesting verses he was always making up. It was an amazing, fabulous home for the cassowaries because when they ventured out of the rainforest, the beach with the sparkling ocean was right there.

Today the sea looked like it was full of shiny, silvery, dazzling diamonds. The beach was full of sand that looked like it had teeny tiny pebbles scattered in funny patterns all over it, as far as the eyes could see. The little crabs that lived on the beach here, cleverly made these little balls of sand as they dug and scrambled around. They would always scurry away to hide so quickly whenever anyone came too near their sand-homes.

Chrissie was very excited. In her family, each year, one of the cute, stripy-feathered chicks had a turn at giving out all of the Christmas treasures. These had all been so thoughtfully brought here by their Mummy Clarissa. She had come back to visit them after being away all year and they were so overjoyed to see each other. This Christmas, it was Chrissie's turn! Her big, loving Daddy, Clementine Cassowary, had chosen an impressive Cassowary Plum Tree to be their Christmas tree, in a nice, shady and sheltered spot in the rainforest. Under this was where Clarissa had made her very special Christmas treasures' nest.

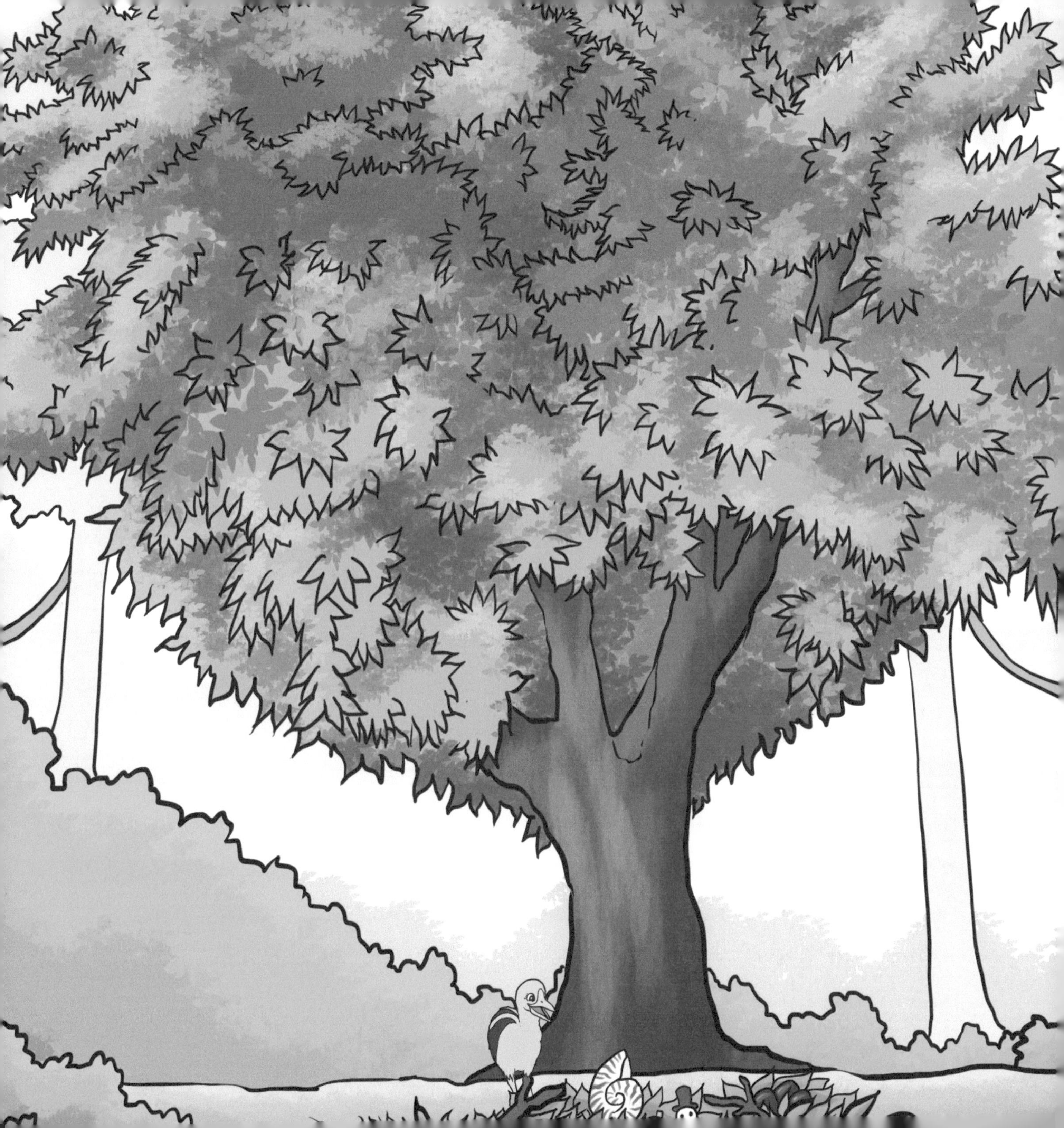

Now, Chrissie had been peeking into the specially made nest every day since Clarissa had lovingly put her gifts in there, covered over with sticks, leaves & branches so that no little cassowary chick's eyes could see them. Chrissie would gaze at them and touch them gently, wondering what was in each one, so cautiously deposited there and hidden out of sight with such care. On this particular day, she was becoming more & more curious. She could just not help herself. She had to uncover & investigate what her present was. So she did just that.

Oh! It was a beautiful big, round, smooth, creamy light pink and brown shell, with beautiful lines & patterns around it, that her Mummy had found in her wanderings. It was called a Nautilus shell. She had kept it for Chrissie because Clementine had told her how much Chrissie just loved their beach walks. She would always bring back pretty shells, ever curiously wondering how they all kept washing up day after day, from who knew where, onto their beach. One side of this shell was smooth and shiny-almost as if it was glowing. It was so unique and it was for her! Plus, there was a bright blue, ripe cassowary plum from the very tree under which the gifts were hidden. "Yum! Mummy knows we all love the fruit off this tree. That's an extra treat!"

Chrissie then thought "I wonder what my brother and sisters' treasures are." She looked closely at them all .She touched each one. She became so curious again that she just had to uncover another, then another and then another. Well, now they were all out in the open. The big, beautiful shell for her and the other treasures too.

For Calvin Cassowary, her funny, bigger brother, there was a bunch of bright red berries in a dark brown, boat-shaped seed pod that Clarissa had found on another interesting beach called Tully Heads . Clarissa loved that special place because it had the sparkly ocean on one side of the beach, a big golden sand bar in the middle stretching out, and then the famous Tully River on the other side of it (where there have been known to be large crocodiles living!) Chrissie knew Calvin would love his gift because he loved to play & float all sorts of things in the shallows at the water's edge when there were no humans to be seen on their beach. There was another bright blue, egg-shaped Cassowary Plum for Calvin too.

The next gift she uncovered (along with another large cassowary plum) was a large, greeny, yellowy, browny, funny looking ball shaped thing. It was made up of all different shaped and sized pieces that could come apart and could be put back together-just like a puzzle. It was a huge seed from the mangroves, the fascinating trees that grew along the Tully riverbanks where Clarissa had travelled.

She had had to be cautious and stay very alert in that muddy, murky area, so that she did not encounter any crocodiles. She had had to swim a little way too, to find exactly what she was looking for, but she did love swimming. She would catch fish for her dinner this way sometimes. This puzzle-seed present was for Claire, who loved building and making things.

The last gift Chrissie had uncovered was Clarissa's present for Cassy Cassowary, the youngest chick in their family. Cassy loved to find and collect sparkly, bright objects. Clarissa knew Cassy would be very excited because one day she had been slowly, carefully crossing the road into Mission Beach, in an area called Lacey's Creek.

She was coming back to visit Clementine and their chicks, when she had stumbled upon a small, beautiful thing on the side of the road, that human ladies sometimes kept in their bags that went over their shoulders. She had seen some of them pull these shiny things out of their bags to look at their own reflection in. Then they often would paint that funny coloured stuff on their lips. Very strange! This little thing (called a 'mirror') had tiny blue and green beads all over the back of it and the front of it was brilliant silver glass. It was a wonderful gift for Cassy to treasure and keep with her collection of shiny things. Chrissie knew she would love it, and she knew Cassy especially loved the juicy, tropical fruits from the tree above. She had one with her gift too.

Now, Chrissie the Curious Cassowary had investigated the last gift from Clarissa, and was thinking that they all looked so interesting and pretty, all different shapes and sizes- just like the chicks. She was just thinking how lucky they all were -and guess what happened?

Mummy Clarissa Cassowary came to check her special nest of treasures with everything all safely hidden away from chicks' curious eyes. What did she discover? She was shocked and aghast to find her carefully hidden gifts all out in plain sight. She let out a big screech! She then noticed Chrissie Cassowary standing right next to the nest, looking very excited and proud of herself. Chrissie gave her Mummy a big, snuggly cuddle to show how much she loved her gift. Clarissa thought to herself: "Oh dear. I should have known Chrissie would do this when it was her turn. She's such a very curious cassowary. Now she will have to help me cover them all back up before the others see them."

So Clarissa explained this to Chrissie, saying: "Do you like it when you get a surprise Chrissie?" Chrissie nodded enthusiastically. Then Clarissa asked her "Do you think Calvin, Claire and Cassy would like to have a nice surprise for Christmas too? How do you think they would feel if there was no surprise for them?" Chrissie nodded again, her eyes getting wider as she thought. She knew they would be terribly disappointed. (Wouldn't you be?)

She started to realise that her curiosity might have caused a big upset to the rest of her family members. She couldn't believe she hadn't been more considerate of them, only thinking about herself.

Clarissa then said "Well, what do you think we need to do, so that their surprise isn't spoiled Chrissie?" "Oh, I need to hide them and cover them all up again so they get their surprises Mummy." "That's a great idea." her Mummy said. "Let's do it together quickly now before anybody's surprise is spoiled." So that's what they did.

While all of this was going on, Chrissie's Grandfather Clem had been watching. He thought he could help Chrissie with her curious ways, because maybe the next time, Mummy or someone else helpful, might not get there in time to stop others being hurt or upset by Chrissie's curiosity. After Clarissa and Chrissie had finished hiding every extraordinary little treasure again, he called Chrissie to come for a walk with him through the rainforest. They found a section of forest where no humans came, and walked slowly, happily together on a track created by their cassowary feet going back and forwards every day as they foraged for their food.

Grandfather Clem said to Chrissie "What was all of that about with your Mummy's gifts Chrissie?" Chrissie hung her head a bit and said in a little voice: "I was so silly Grandfather Clem. I was too curious, like I always am. My curiosity nearly spoiled my brother and sisters' Christmas surprises. I almost upset my Mummy a lot because they were her presents she so lovingly brought for each of us. I'm feeling very sad now." There were even little tears in her eyes as she told her Grandfather what happened.

Clem Cassowary was a very clever old bird. He knew he had a way that he could help Chrissie. He said to her "Chrissie, there's nothing wrong with being a curious cassowary. In fact, it's a great way to become very smart, because you're always wanting to find things out and asking questions. That's terrific! It's just when your curiosity makes you so curious that you don't think of others' needs and care about others that it's a problem. Is that right?" "Yes, Grandfather Clem, that's exactly right. What am I going to do?" asked Chrissie. "Well", said Clem "you could use your magic brain to help you."

"My magic brain? Grandfather, what's a magic brain? That sounds exciting! Tell me, tell me please?" begged Chrissie. She nearly tripped over a tree root in her curious excitement at the thought of a 'magic brain'. Clem laughed. "It is your own clever brain, helping you with finding the right words to say to help you with any problems or challenges you're facing Chrissie. Our brains are so clever, that I always call them our 'Magic Brains'.

"Wow! That sounds great Grandfather. How do I use my 'Magic Brain' then? How? Can I start using mine right now?" Chrissie urged him. He answered her "Yes, you sure can Chrissie. Let's work out what you can do. Do you have something you want to change about yourself?" She thought about that, then said to him "I know! I don't want to be so curious that I hurt others, Grandfather." she told him. "Ok" he said. "What do you want instead?" She thought, and then said happily "I want to be a caring and considerate cassowary, not just a curious cassowary!"

So Grandfather Clem said to her: "That's wonderful Chrissie! Now we use our ' Magic Brains' to make up a verse together, with words that help you with that. Then we feed our magic brains with those words over and over every day, at least 10 times, morning and night, out aloud. This is what makes our brains really magic-saying these good things over and over and over. Then our brains become so 'magic', that they work to make the good things come true for us!"

"Really?" asked Chrissie in curious wonder. 'Yes, Chrissie, it really works! Let's ask our magic brains right now to help us with some great words to help you with your wish to be more caring and considerate then."

Clem and Chrissie walked and talked, working it all out. This is what they created:

"I used to be so curious,
As curious as could be.
I just had to see everything,
Even if it not for me.
It is ok to be curious,
In fact it's rather cool.

We can show we're really smart,
When we're curious at school.
Now I'm a lot more caring,
As caring as I can be,
Because then that helps everyone-
I'm a caring, considerate me!"

Chrissie and Grandfather Clem walked contentedly together back to their family. They said the words over and over to help Chrissie remember them. Clem Cassowary reminded her that what really made the magic work in our brains was to say the same, positive verse-words out loud to yourself, 10 times, always in the morning when you first wake up, and every night before you go off to your dreamyland, recovery sleep.

Clem told her that another thing that made our brain so magic, was that it never goes to sleep! Even when we sleep, it's always working to help you with the things you told it you wanted. It was pretty incredible!

Chrissie was so excited about her magic brain and so thankful to her Grandfather Clem. Everyday she said her verse just like he'd suggested, morning & night, because he had also told her that it was up to her if she really wanted to achieve these things. Nobody else could do it for her. That was the very special secret.

She wanted to be more caring and considerate, so she did this: She said her verse over and over, mornings and nights. She became more and more caring and considerate to everyone around her, every day. Everyone noticed, especially herself. She had done it! She had changed by using her magic brain's wonderful powers.

She taught all of her brother and sister chicks how to use their magic brains too. (I wonder what each of them might have wanted to achieve or become? What do you think? What could you use yours for?)

That Christmas, under the amazing rainforest tree called the Cassowary Plum that Daddy Clementine had chosen, , they held a happy little ceremony, their whole family gathered together. Each of the chicks had made their own choice of a type of seed pod to give as their Christmas gift to Mummy, Daddy and Grandfather. They had each scratched their own design carefully into the seed pod for them to keep. That was tradition in their Cassowary family. These little gifts were very highly treasured by all of the adults, because they were so individual and distinctive.

Next, each of the unique, lovingly hidden treasures from Mummy Clarissa Cassowary, were uncovered so carefully by Chrissie, this year's Christmas Cassowary. To Calvin, she passed the berry seed-pod boat for him to play with and float. He was very excited and couldn't wait. For Claire, the mangrove puzzle-ball seed was handed to her with great care, so it did not break apart until she was ready to do this puzzle herself. She looked at it with wonder and thought how could her Mummy know such a gift would be so terrific for her. (She couldn't wait to see how tricky this puzzle ball would be. The trickier the better, she thought.)

Cassy Cassowary, the baby of the family, squealed with delight when Chrissie presented her with the beautiful little, blue and green beaded, shiny mirror. It was perfect for her collection.

Then she squealed again, because she caught site of herself in the smooth glassy side of it- how very exciting! She let everyone have a look at themselves in her little mirror too. There were more squeals of surprise and fun. They all loved their lush, ripe, beautiful, pretty blue cassowary plums too-delicious!

Chrissie was smiling and thinking through all of this, how extremely glad she was, that her Mummy's gifts, each one so caringly thought out and just right, had indeed stayed hidden to become the surprises they were today. She gave her Mummy a very special, warm look. To her surprise and delight, her Mummy had something for her. She had been so happy seeing her brother and sister cassowary chicks receiving their presents, that she had forgotten all about the last gift in the nest. She was having a surprise after all too!

This gift was of course Mummy Clarissa Cassowary's special treasure for Chrissie. Clarissa had known the impressive nautilus shell would be just perfect for their curious Chrissie who loved the things that washed up on their beach. Clarissa slowly, gently uncovered this one & she and Daddy Clementine Cassowary together handed it to Chrissie, with so much love in their hearts and eyes for her.

Clarissa said to Chrissie "Thank you for being such a wonderful Christmas Cassowary Chrissie. Well done. We are so proud of you and how you have been using your magic brain to work on yourself and for helping Calvin, Claire & Cassy to use theirs too. What a special, giving cassowary you are. Now you have become our "Chrissy the Curious, most Caringly Considerate Cassowary." Chrissie was feeling so pleased and blessed. She gave all of her family members a very special, warm Christmas hug each. She did give her Grandfather Clem an extra specially long Christmas hug, to thank him for the very best, most precious gift of all: her incredible 'Magic Brain'.

Praise for Kristina Cone's first children's empowering story book

Kristina Cone has thrown her considerable experience and talent into "Timmy The Terribly Tired Tiger Cub".

What a great way for parents to pass on some wonderful life lessons, while entertaining their children (and themselves) at the same time!

I can see this book being enjoyed over and over again by families.

I recommend "Timmy The Terribly Tired Tiger Cub" to all families, and hope they enjoy it as much as my family has.

-Stuart Edwards
Deputy Principal,
Bentley Park College, Cairns

leave only footprints

Printed in the United States
By Bookmasters